figure it out

the *real* woman's GUIDE TO GREAT STYLE

figure*it*out

the *real* woman's GUIDE TO GREAT STYLE

from the editors of *figure*™ *magazine*
Geri Brin and **Tish Jett**
with Joanna Goddard

photographs by
Vincent Ricardel

Editorial Director
Trisha Malcolm

Art Director
Janine Bily

Stylists
Desiree Konian
Leetoya Casey

Photographer
Vince Ricardel

Illustrations
Marilena Perilli

Editor
Joanna Goddard

Book Division Manager
Michelle Lo

Production Manager
David Joinnides

President and Publisher, Sixth&Spring Books
Art Joinnides

ISBN 0-7394-4553-7

Manufactured in USA

sixth&spring
books

welcome
to the

Dear Friend,

Fashion genes don't come along with DNA for curly hair, freckles and height. There's one thing we have to cultivate totally by ourselves: style. Each of us must figure out our special signature look, what flatters our individual curves, makes us feel confident and comfortable and best expresses our inner loveliness.

We're bombarded with fashion options everywhere we turn, but turning to the right place for sound advice isn't always easy. Will your best friend tell you your bottom looks way too big in the slacks you adore? Will your husband be honest when you ask if a sweater hides your midriff bulge? And can you really look at yourself objectively?

Your Style Guide

Congratulations. By picking up *figure it out*, fabulous style is at your fingertips.

Every day, millions of women stand in front of their closets asking, "What should I wear?"

Not any more. Finished, over, done. You're now in control of your own destiny, and it all starts first thing in the morning when you get dressed.

Figure it out is written to be an entertaining, informative style guide just for you. We'll demonstrate what to wear and what not to wear—taking you from mundane to marvelous in eight concise and constructive chapters.

The chapters address every occasion in your life—work, play, a night on the town, a day at the beach, a romantic evening at home, and more—demonstrating exactly how to dress well for each situation. Every chapter opens with a perfect look and ends with an appropriate and inappropriate way to dress.

Remember, each woman's figure is unique, so not every rule in this book will apply across the board. For example, turtlenecks look smarter on women with long, shapely necks than on those who are overly endowed in the chin department. And tunics lay better on smaller, flatter backsides than on more pronounced derrieres.

real world

Look Good, Feel Great

Our philosophy is simple: when you look good, you feel fabulous. You radiate a sense of happiness and well being, and the world sees you as a woman of style and substance. People are drawn to you and want to be around you. Women want to chat with you over coffee, men want to take you to dinner, bosses want to entrust you with projects. With style comes confidence, and the world opens up.

"Wait a minute," you may say. "This all sounds fine and good, but it's not so easy to pull off style day after day in the real world." You're tired, you're stressed, you're over-worked. Besides, who has the time to worry about being stylish?

Our answer? We're here to help. We'll reveal the secrets of smooth lines and elegant shapes. We'll give you constructive, down-to-earth, concrete steps to revealing your true beauty. We'll help you find your look, express yourself and, most of all, build confidence. After all, that's what style is all about.

Defining Style

Style is not a matter of charge cards and expense accounts. Whether you're a penny pincher or a high roller, a spender or a saver, you can look great. Style can be creative and simple. For example, a crisp white shirt and faded jeans paired with dangly earrings and a silky scarf will suddenly take you on a *Roman Holiday*, without ever leaving home.

Style is not about the latest designers, seasonal fads or what's in or out in a fickle fashion moment. Looking great has nothing to do with trends, and everything to do with classic lines and flattering fit. We'll focus on accentuating your best features and developing a timeless look.

Three Trusted Tips

Getting dressed every day may not be the most important thing you do in your life. It should, however, be way up there on your list of top priorities. Keep the following three tips in mind as you dress:

1. If you don't already own one, rush out this instant and buy a full-length mirror. It will be the most valuable fashion investment you will ever make. Your full-length mirror will become your new best friend: never leave home without a quick heart to heart.

2. Forget about sizes once and for all. The numbers on the tags have no importance—repeat that over and over until you believe it. Every designer and manufacturer cuts clothes differently. You may range up to four sizes depending on where you shop. Take two or three sizes into the dressing room unless you already know how a certain label fits you. Buy clothes that fit, not that you hope to squeeze into next summer or that are too loose to flatter your figure.

3. Every woman should have a tailor. This minor cost will provide a major benefit: impeccable fit. How many times have you suffered with jeans that hug your hips perfectly, but sag around your waist? Wouldn't it be nice if your new blazer accentuated your curves instead of falling straight down? We're better served by fewer clothes that fit well than lots of items that don't quite work. So let the tailor work his or her magic, and people will wonder how you always manage to look so fabulous.

Know Thyself

Style is all about you, so it's important to know yourself, your face and your figure.

Ask yourself the following questions:

What are my three best features?

When I picture myself, what am I wearing?

What are my favorite outfits?

If I could take one woman's style, who would she be?

When people tell me that I look nice, am I typically wearing a certain color or outfit?

How do colors make me feel? (What is my favorite color? What color is my bedroom? What colors look good with my skin tone?)

Now look through magazines and tear out pages with clothes you love and that you could see yourself wearing. You'll start to get a sense of your personal style. You can even keep a dressing journal to list your favorite things, including accessories and a "wish list" of items that would help complete your wardrobe. Put your pictures in your journal for quick reference.

Skeletons In Your Closet

We all have certain pieces that work beautifully: that cozy turtleneck sweater, that slinky pink camisole, those perfectly faded jeans. But lurking behind these much-loved pieces are cringe-worthy fashion bombs that you can't believe you let into your home. A pink mohair blazer? Lime green asymmetrical top? Tapered stretch pants? Yikes. What on earth were you thinking?

If your closet is littered with clothes you never wear, instead of things you love, it's time to take stock. When you peruse the racks in your closet, ask yourself: how many of these clothes do I really wear?

Take this simple test: Stand in front of your closet and pull out the clothes you wear all the time. Don't compromise. Don't include pieces gathering dust or those you swear you'll wear someday. (If you haven't already, chances are you won't.)

Next, organize these clothes by categories: office, weekend, special occasion and so on. Do you see a pattern emerging here—in color, cut, or design? Do you have a stack of crisp button-down shirts? Do you prefer warm wool sweaters? Do you express yourself with bright, cheerful colors? Your personal style may be hiding in your very own closet.

Now here comes the hard part. If the clothes you never wear take up precious space, if they don't make you feel wonderful and confident, if they're beyond salvation by your tailor—dump them. Give them to friends or relatives. And move on.

Cleaning your closet will help you take account of your wardrobe and evolve with style. (And at the very least, it's good *feng shui*.)

The Best Part: Go Shopping

Armed with the knowledge that you look terrific in flat-front pants with a touch of stretch, A-line skirts that skim your knees, and jackets that nip in at your waist, you can embark on a true treasure hunt the next time you go shopping.

Be disciplined. Look for the pieces you know will make you look stunning, and don't compromise your style standards. Having certain signature pieces in no way limits your imagination and creativity in putting together your look. It's liberating to finally know what really works every time. Your flair and imagination can add the zest to the rest—signature accessories, wonderful fabrics, the twist of a scarf, the color of your lipstick.

The Last Word

We truly believe all women are gorgeous. We'll help your clothes match your inner beauty, with great classic pieces and true, timeless style.

We hope *figure it out* will become a favored companion that you can turn to again and again for counsel and comfort, and will help you see that looking stylish can be one of life's greatest little pleasures.

Enjoy!

Geri and Tish

which
BODY TYPE
are YOU?

To dress well, you have to understand your body. Our proportions vary in natural and common ways, and every woman's body falls into one of several shapes. A woman's body type will generally influence which fit is right for her, so once you figure out your type, you can find the styles that are best for you—and feel more confident about your look and yourself.

The first step: figure out which body type you have—H, O, A or X.*

The second step: read this book.

We feature eight gorgeous women who—from tall to short, with flabby arms to full thighs—embody the figure problems every woman faces to one degree or another. By understanding their bodies, they know which clothes and styles make them look great.

The women will be wearing "Dos" and "Don'ts" for every occasion—from weekends to workouts to the workplace.

Next to each picture, we've placed icons (H, O, A or X). If your body type is not crossed out, you'll love that look. But if your body type is crossed out, you should shun that style.

When the "Dos" and "Don'ts" target traits that have nothing to do with the form of one's body (such as arms or necks), we don't use the HOAX icons. Similarly, chapter 7 and chapter 8 discuss lingerie and accessories, so the tips pertain to everyone, and we don't need the HOAX system.

Ready to go? Let's figure it out!

*Mary Duffy, a former fashion model, developed the HOAX Fashion Formula in the eighties to help women identify their body types and select the fashions that will look best on them. As the creator of a plus-size line for Simplicity Pattern Co., Duffy was one of the first designers to address the needs of full-figured sewers. HOAX is a T.M. of Mary Duffy.

If you're an "H"

Your hips are no more than two inches wider than your bust.

Your waist is somewhat undefined.

Your shoulders and back are average to wide.

This is the easiest body type to dress, due to overall good proportions.

H

If you're on "O"

Your upper body is fuller than your lower body.

From side view, your central oval (bust, midriff and tummy) is protuberant.

Your hips, thighs and legs appear relatively slender.

Your neck, face and back of the neck may be prone to fullness.

O

If you're an "A"

Your lower body is clearly fuller than your upper body.

From front view, your thighs are the widest part of your anatomy.

Your bust and shoulders may seem narrow compared to the rest of your body.

This is the most common body shape.

A

If you're an "X"

You have a full bust, round hip line and clearly defined waist.

You may have extra fullness in the upper arms and thighs.

Your figure is womanly.

This body type can sometimes be challenging to dress since it's difficult to drape fabric on curved lines.

X

workingitout

Whether we sit behind a desk, stand before a class or drive from client to client, we always like to look our best at work.

Stylish, well-fitting clothes do more than build our confidence. They can actually play a role in advancing our careers and earning us respect.

Even in ultra-casual work environments, there are rules we must follow: Cover our cleavage, skip the stilettos and leave the fishnet tights at home. And in strictly professional offices, we can still manage to reflect our individual styles. Enhance a basic black pant suit with a color saturated scarf; team a gorgeous silky blouse with a long, slim skirt.

It's always safe to choose classic pieces that accentuate the positive and eliminate the negative. Let your lovely legs peak from beneath a merino wool skirt. Show off your divine waistline with a wrap dress.

A final note: Choose your work outfit before retiring for the night. Make sure everything is clean and neatly pressed, and pick out your bag and jewelry. (After all, who can concentrate on accessories first thing in the morning?) Then you can climb into bed with the knowledge that you'll get an extra fifteen minutes of sleep every day for the rest of the week. Sweet dreams!

double
trouble

If you've got it,
don't flaunt it in
double-breasted
clothes. The two
rows of buttons
might give your
small-busted friends
more up front, but
you've got enough
without them. And
long clearly is wrong.

Wrapped jersey is a big bust's best friend because it drapes gently over the body and forms the perfect V shape to flatter every curve. A shorter skirt puts it all in proportion.

wrap it up

waist not, want not

Shapeless jackets make you look…
shapeless. Duh! Curves deserve more.

waisted

Caress a winsome waist
with a form-fitting jacket.

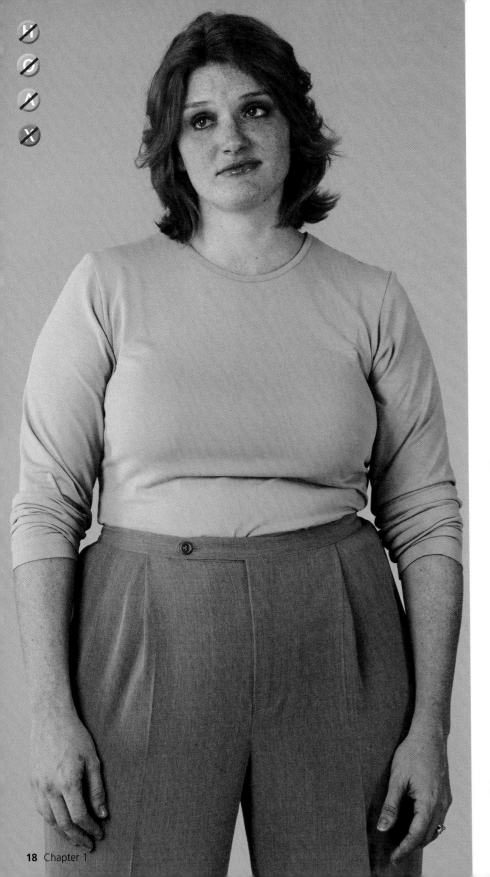

Pleats are absolute no-no's for tummies, something like arrows pointing right to the problem.

fattening

flattening

Flat fronts are flattering.
That's all you need to know.

ruff
ruff

Rows of big ruffles planted smack dab on a bountiful bosom—and buttons clear up to the neck—are certainly not good things, even with vertical stripes.

A tiny ruffle around a scooped neck is figure flattering. So are little ties that wrap the wrist.

meow meow

hip hip

Trying to hide well-endowed hips and butt with a shapeless long sweater is like wearing a string bikini. It draws attention just where you don't want it.

hooray

Vertical ribs above the hips are well… hip…and make you look longer and leaner.

arm
wrestling

If your arms aren't your favorite
limbs, why for goodness sake
would you surround them with
a tight-fitting, cap-sleeved
turtleneck sweater?

Cover ample arms
so everyone sees
your wonderful face.

well armed

stretching the truth

Oh, that pesky hip/thigh issue. Don't address it with too much stretch and not enough skirt.

the final
stretch

Skim over your problems
with slim, knee-length skirts
with a soupçon of stretch.

You can run, but you can't hide. Contrary to popular opinion, clothes that hang limply on the body—even long black clothes—often say big and dumpy.

undercover

well suited

Subtle suits with skirts that kiss the knee and jackets that give a little pinch at the waist put the hips in their proper place, away from the center of attention.

bulking up

Layering can be stylish, but bulky sweater over bulky sweater can be bulk to the second power. Warm maybe, but definitely not chic.

thinning
out

Thin knitted layers over a bigger
body say posed and polished.

short
cuts

It's too tight. It's too short. It's definitely not a good look for the office.

skirting the issue

A+ for A-line skirts that point to pretty calves teamed with matching body-sliding jackets.

inappropriate

Oops, someone forgot her blouse.

We got the account.

appropriate

relaxation techniques

The weekend may be the time to kick off your heels, kick up your heels and let down your hair, but does that mean you can't look pulled together all the same?

Style shouldn't take weekend vacations. Being fashionable is an ongoing process, a way to express your personality no matter what the circumstances, no matter what time of day or night. What possible satisfaction comes from grabbing a huge, baggy T-shirt and faded sweats to work out, or worse yet to go to the grocery store? Comfort, you say. Nonsense, we say.

It's just as easy and infinitely more satisfying to make a tiny effort. How about a pair of jeans, a neat T-shirt, and a tweed jacket? As for workouts — from yoga to walking to kick-boxing — the choices have never been so varied and so attractive. Why would you deprive yourself of these pleasures?

Looking good should be a point of pride all the time since your clothes and grooming reflect what you think of yourself. Don't believe for an instant that the rest of the world doesn't pick up that message — even on weekends and in the gym.

A final note: It's a sad but true commentary on our times that our skinny sisters can manage to look fairly decent and unkempt at the same time. We think that all women should make the effort to look great every single day.

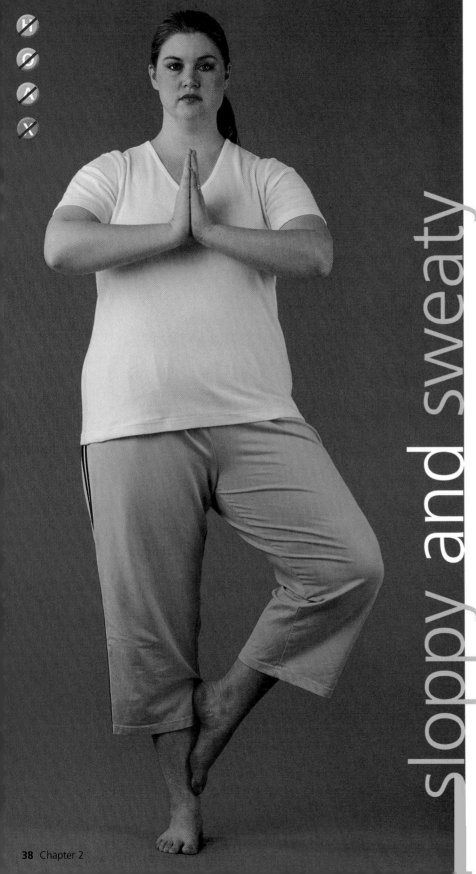

sloppy and sweaty

Sloppy sweats and over-sized tees hugging an O-shaped figure not only say "I don't care," they also prevent the body from moving fluidly when you need it to. Besides, you never know who you're going to run into at the gym.

don't
sweat it

Serious pieces specifically
designed for exercise
and yoga have just the
right amount of stretch
so they move with you
and flatter the shape at
the same time.

Tight-waist, low-rise bottoms and abbreviated tops may look cute on the hanger, but they're anything but cute hanging around a tummy with even the slightest bulge.

tummy
ache

yummy for the tummy

When well-fitting jeans (sitting comfortably just below the waist) meet a sweater without producing a skin show, they make beautiful music together.

up to your ears

Turtlenecks are like magicians on short necks—they make them disappear— and when they're sleeveless turtles, they do nothing whatsoever for ample arms.

an open find

The wide open space of a V-neck paired with well-fitted sleeves elongates the neck and shapes big arms.

fuss
pot

Oversized pockets on the side, a big zipper up the middle and heavy fabric don't make a jean skirt— or any other skirt—your figure's best friend. (An oversized shirt could save the day.)

clean and clear

A belted waist and clean lines define the waist while a slight
funnel shape adds a little feminine detail above the boots.

big deal

Huge, shapeless, heavy knit sweaters on women with large breasts and big stomachs make them look like women with large breasts and big stomachs.

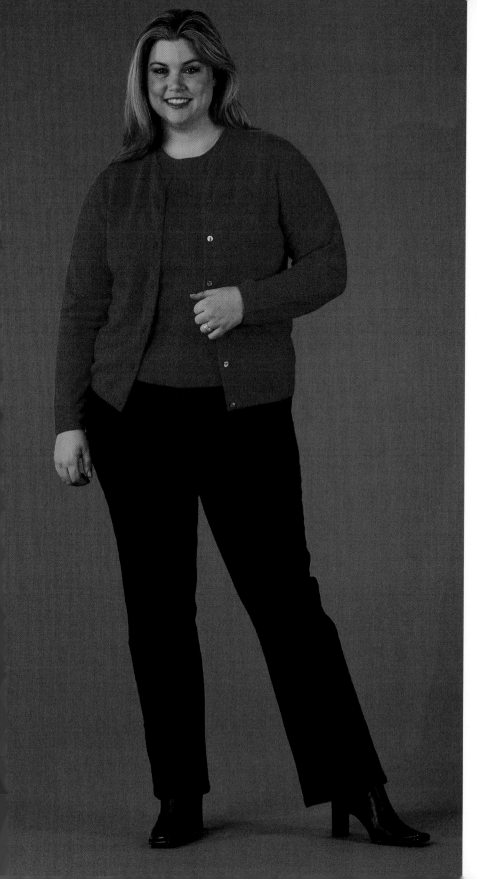

Fine wools may be more expensive than other yarns, but they provide more warmth and drape naturally and beautifully. Choose a luscious color to show you have nothing to hide.

H
O
A
X

a hot number

out of shape

A top without support and a constricting bottom don't make for a winning workout wardrobe.

Coordinates that are comfortable, functional and flattering are knockouts in and out of the gym.

knockout!

top off

Everyone wants a fun top or two in her wardrobe, but when its peek-a-boo details emphasize heavy arms and it pulls tightly across the bust, what fun is that?

A top should skim
your chest instead
of smothering it.
Roomy flounced
sleeves cover
upper arms
and emphasize
pretty hands.

weighting
lines

Wide stripes are always cool looking, but when they're horizontal, they rarely do anything more than take away the pretty curves and emphasize the hips.

You can have your stripes and your figure too. The collar lights up the face and the three-quarter sleeves with turned-up cuffs show off just the right amount of arm.

great lines

inappropriate

You're not going out
of the house, right?

Good to go.

appropriate

onthetown

What's as much fun as a night out with the girls, a swanky party or a dreamy date? Choosing the clothes you're going to wear, of course. Who doesn't love slipping into a flounced skirt that moves with your curves, pulling on sexy tights that make your legs look ravishing and spritzing on heavenly perfume that stays behind when you leave the room?

Whether you're going to a restaurant, club, theater or party, your wardrobe choices are extensive, guided principally by what flatters your figure. Your clothes create first impressions and speak volumes about your intentions. You want to look sexy, tender, demure or mysterious? Go for it.

Be careful not to slide down the slippery slope and turn terrific into tarty or stunning into sleazy. Putting a pink bra under a black transparent blouse isn't cute, no matter how trendy you've heard it is.

You've got a delicious décolleté? Give us a peek, not a panorama. Have ample arms? Don't flaunt them; wear a jacket over your bustier, throw a shawl around your shoulders, slip a transparent blouse over your camisole. It's as easy as that.

A final note: You should always have one foolproof party frock in your closet for last-minute invitations. Who knows when you'll be invited to a fabulous soiree at a moment's notice. Wait, is that the phone ringing?

Shiny is nice on apples, patent leather shoes and diamonds, not on your stomach or boobs. Even if the rest works, shiny still doesn't cut it.

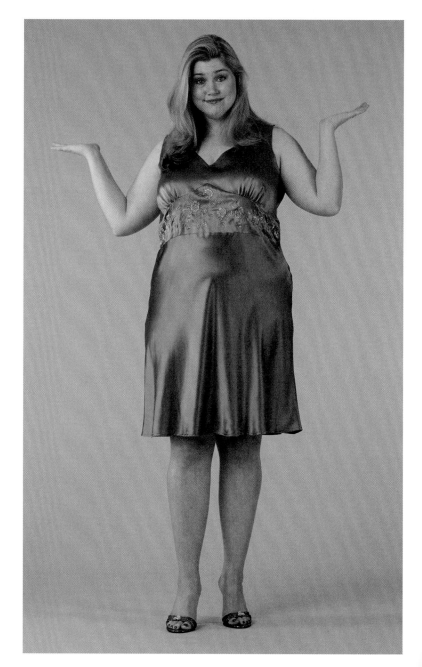

a shining example

a stunning statement

Va-va-voom to soft fluid jersey falling just below the knee and draping into a wide and low V at the top.

strike out the band

A bottom band surrounding full hips is like a posse surrounding the outlaw. You'll never get away with it.

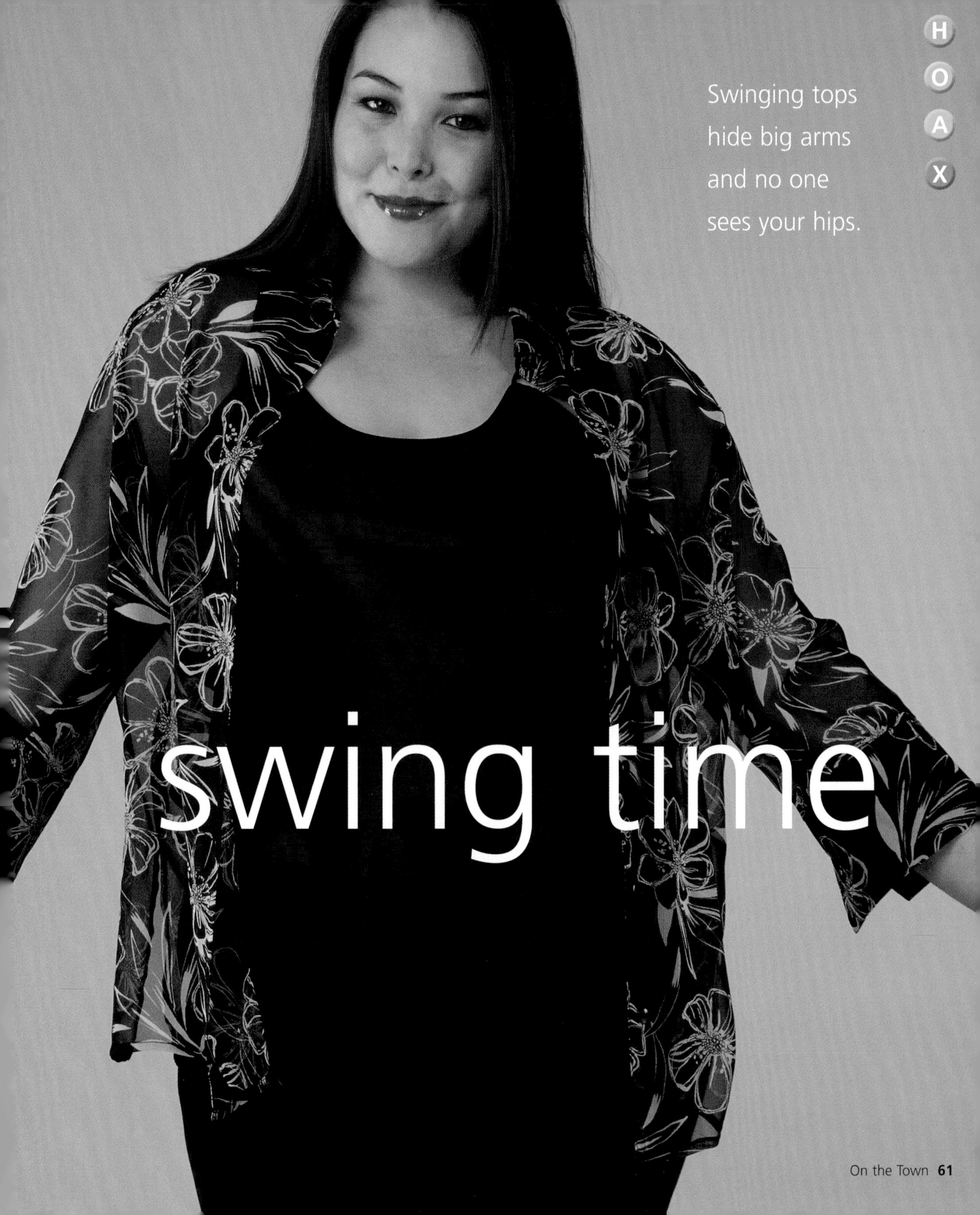

H O A X

Swinging tops hide big arms and no one sees your hips.

swing time

shelve it

If you don't like your arms, why would you wrap them with silly little buckles or bows?

Loose-fitting short sleeves with a tad of shoulder pad make larger arms look smaller.

shoulder it

weighty
matters

What could possibly be going through your mind when you choose an outfit that's louder than a marching band down Main Street? When the two pieces march together, your middle knows no limits.

Colors in the same family usually get along well, particularly if the bottom is darker than the top. Furthermore, floating fabrics will give you a lighter look.

light subjects

hide out

When you don't really
have anything to hide,
why hide behind a super
voluminous dress?

wrap it up

Sultry wraps are kind
to curves since they
let you control their fit
over the waist, hips
and bottom and how
low to go at the neck.

belt it out

You'll know a belted dress doesn't work for you if it exaggerates the difference between your waist and your hips.

Take the A line if you have a defined waist and a significant top and bottom.

curves
ahead

easy doesn't do it

Almost doesn't count. If it doesn't have a shape and doesn't quite touch down on your curves, it won't be your best look.

bosom buddy

An empire waist is a bosom's best buddy, especially if it ties at the bust line and draws attention to your great shape.

Great shoulders and décolletage deserve star treatment, not straps that pinch and a shape that obliterates the bust.

ouch

Ahhh

Corset tops show off sumptuous shoulders and highlight the bosom, not to mention control midriff bulge.

The last thing an X-shaped figure needs is pleats spewing over the hips, a tie at the waist and a square neck with wide straps.

alice in wonderland

wonderland

Slim strapless columns
make for slim silhouettes.

inappropriate

Like my pink bra?

appropriate

Bra be gone.

onoccasion

Even before we get the "official" invitation to a special occasion, we start obsessing about what we're going to wear. Reversely, how many times are we thrown into a tizzy when an unexpected invitation arrives and we realize we have "absolutely nothing" to wear.

When it comes to special events, we should take a tip from the Girl Scouts: "Be Prepared." Organize your special-occasion wardrobe long before invitations arrive. Then you can look forward to the revelry and skip the panicked, last-minute dash to the mall.

Building a special-occasion reserve can be as simple as adding a long skirt, a special jacket and some fancy tops to your wardrobe. Another option is to get a short sleek dress and a long formal dress, each with a matching jacket or shawl. Elegant pantsuits also can be wonderful choices, as long as the cut, fabric and embellishments fit the occasion.

If you're out shopping and see something that you love, makes you look like a knock-out, and would be perfect for several different events, consider getting it right then even if you have no events on your social calendar at the time.

A final note: Modesty *is* a virtue. At a wedding, wait to flaunt your exquisite cleavage until after the couple is married and then don't let it cascade onto the dining table. At a cocktail party, make sure not to wobble around in too-high heels and a too-short dress. A little bit of pizazz usually goes a long way.

white
out

White isn't right when it's atop big hips and a dark skirt because it makes you look shorter and wider.

white on

Don't be afraid of
whites and pastels. If
the suit fits, wear it.

short shrift

Just because they're made of crepe and show off your legs doesn't mean they help your hips and belong at your cousin's wedding.

lean on me

When it's long
and lithe, no
one will notice
your hips or
your thighs.

am I blue?

Great forms don't
look great in dresses
without great form.

fit to be tried

A fine fitting knit forgives just about every figure and can be one of the best finds in all of fashiondom.

pleating
guilty

No pleats please
if you want to
hide your hips.

hail to the halter

Halter-top dresses work wonders for women with busts, waists and hips.

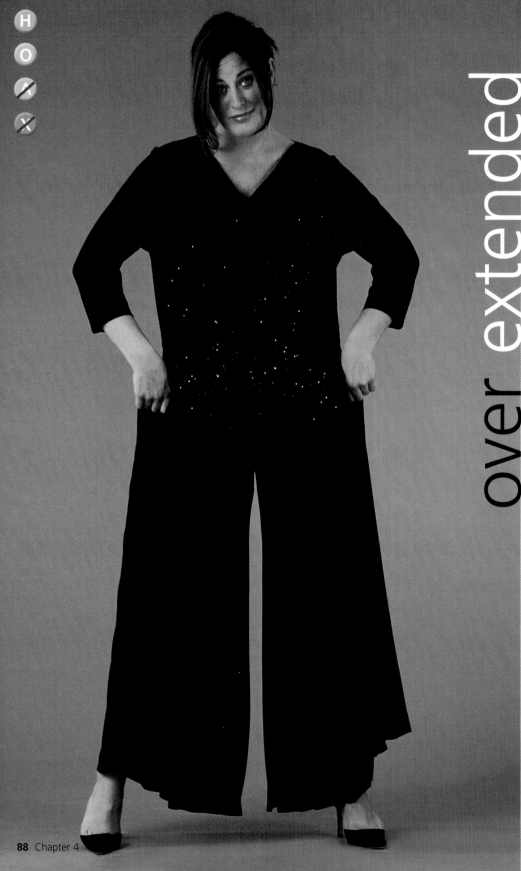

over extended

When there is way too much fabric it looks like there is way too much woman.

less is
more

Paring down with neat,
crisp pieces plays up a
beautiful X-shaped figure.

tied
down

Drawstring pants just
draw attention to
stomachs and hips.

style
of
capri

Wrap tops and capris—
in calm complementary
colors—work wonders
on thicker waists.

middle marker

Double-breasted
suits make curvy
women even
bigger and bustier.

Filmy fabrics
shaped into tunics
and full-cut pants
are godsends for
tummies and
buxom bosoms.

magic
maker

horizontally
challenged

Too short, too tight,
too many horizontal
lines. Just don't do it.

what a line

The right length, the right line, the right color: the right dress. Just do it.

inappropriate

Thanks for sharing –
way, way too much.

Sexy without pushing it.

appropriate

braving the elements

Certainly you don't think that sleet, snow, showers and freezing temperatures are excuses for hiding under dreary, dowdy and dumpy coats.

Outerwear can be dependable and stylish, and no wardrobe is complete without it. Coats and jackets that protect us against the elements should flatter us as much as the clothes beneath.

Many of the same rules apply to outerwear as to other apparel:

If you have a big bust, forget about double-breasted coats.

Don't cinch a trench-coat belt around your waist if you have a tummy.

Don't try to hide in volumes of fabric falling to your ankles if you have a big bottom.

Try a single-breasted three-quarter or seven-eighth-length coat with a clean, loose straight cut.

You mustn't be afraid of color. If it's gray outside, a bright pink rain jacket will make you happy. (Curiously, wearing the same pink dress day after day makes everyone wonder if you're color blind, while wearing a pink coat day after day makes everyone think you've got great style.)

A final note: If your coat collection is composed mainly of investment classics in dark or neutral colors, brighten them up with colorful scarves, vivid hued gloves, a snappy primary colored rain hat and a pair of school-bus-yellow rubber boots.

foul-weather foe

Buttoned to the neck, double-breasted and cinched at the waist, trench coats turn well-endowed bust-lines into big blobs.

foul-
weather
friend

Raglan-sleeves and
swingy silhouettes
look graceful on
almost any figure
and have a
dressed up feel.

furget
about it

This isn't anyone's definition of fun fur. It bulks you up, lops off the top of your body and exposes your midriff. Bury the beast.

just
fur
fun

Faux fur can be
funky, fabulous
and flattering.

drive
on by

Leave snug, double-breasted car coats in the car, especially when they're too short and dissect the body so it resembles a square.

zip, zip
hooray

Long and lean coats with zip-fronts give any body a good look, but make sure your butt doesn't force the fabric to ride up.

Coats that are too short and have drawstrings around the hips can make you look like a stuffed sausage—black or no black.

all stuffed up

Even pink can make you look perfect if it's on a three-quarter-length coat with a straight—but not strict—slimming cut.

pretty in pink

boxed up

Sack-shaped blousons are more flattering on skinny gals, not on real woman with curves in all the right places.

Flaps can be flattering
on the chest when
they line up with
waist-defining pockets.

pick pockets

under the big top

Tents belong in the circus, not on you, especially if you have a short neck and a big bust. (The yards of fabric might look good on a sofa though.)

Body-skimming
Chesterfields
skim over all the
appropriate curves.

coat du jour

under wraps

Even if it does hide the backside, too much leather (or any other inflexible material) can make a woman look shorter, awkward and uncomfortable.

tall
order

Spencer-like jackets
can say tall.

inappropriate

A little short
on substance.

Long and lovely.

appropriate

onthebeach

Oooooh. Or should we say ouch? Shopping for swimwear is every woman's favorite pastime, right up there with root canals and visits to the gynecologist.

Ok, breathe deeply. No matter what your size or shape, you can look fabulous at the beach. The same rules work here as in any other dressing situation. The perfect swimsuit is out there if you know how to find it. Yes, yes, we know there's less to work with and not much room to hide, but you'll be surprised at what a swimsuit with lots of stretch, built-in controls and enhancements can do for your figure. And just remember three magic words: strategic color blocking.

Disregard the size labels on swimwear. It's common to wear a size larger in a swimsuit than in your clothes. Here's a tip: When trying on a suit, stretch your arms, sit down in a chair and bend over. Watch carefully in the three-way mirror to see how the suit moves. If it slips into all the wrong places, continue looking. If it fits comfortably and moves with your body, then you've found yourself a bathing beauty.

A final note: Buy a sexy sarong in a beautiful color or pattern to make you feel comfortably covered-up. Forget about being tied to your beach chair; you'll be able to stroll around confidently, and check out the surf. And who wants to swathe themselves in a bulky beach towel when taking the children to the snack bar? (For chilly summer evenings, a sarong can also work as a pretty shawl.)

Horizontally striped tankinis are designed for teenage waifs, not for women with stomachs, hips or breasts larger than a B cup.

tank it

take it

Solid tankinis with halter tops and moderately high-cut legs help create taller, slimmer silhouettes.

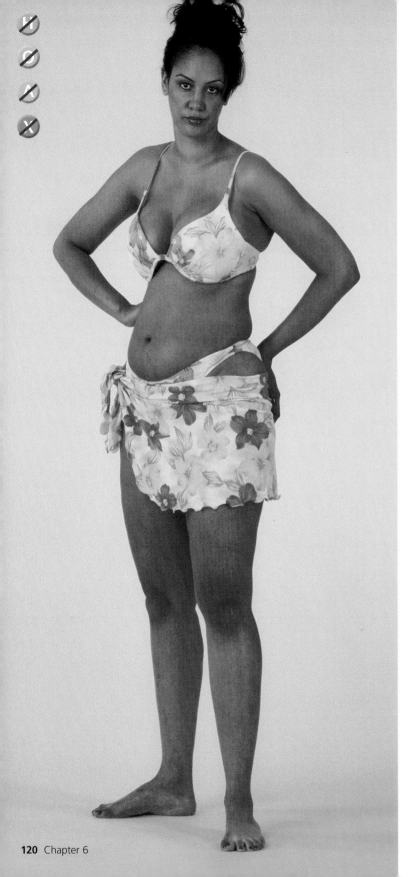

belly up

Sarongs are supposed to cover you up when you're not sunning or swimming. So don't even think of wearing one that's low cut and belly bearing or too short to cover even slightly heavy legs and thighs.

tummy tuck

A sarong that's tied at the waist
downplays the tummy while the
longer length highlights long legs.

maillot my!

A maillot with no support
is like Champagne with no
fizz: flat and amorphous.

smooth
sailing

Inner bras lift the breasts and serious stretch smoothes the body all the way to the top of the thighs.

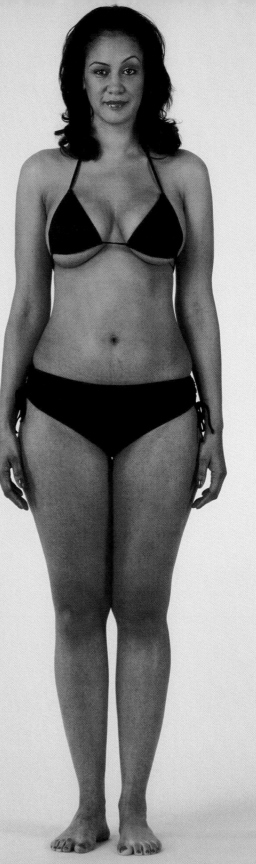

fallout

If you're going to
wear a bikini,
make sure it fits.
Voluptuously round
breasts need to be
contained; itsy-bitsy
fabric triangles are
not up to the job.

fall in

Bodacious busts stay put in halter tops. You can even swim without fear of fallout.

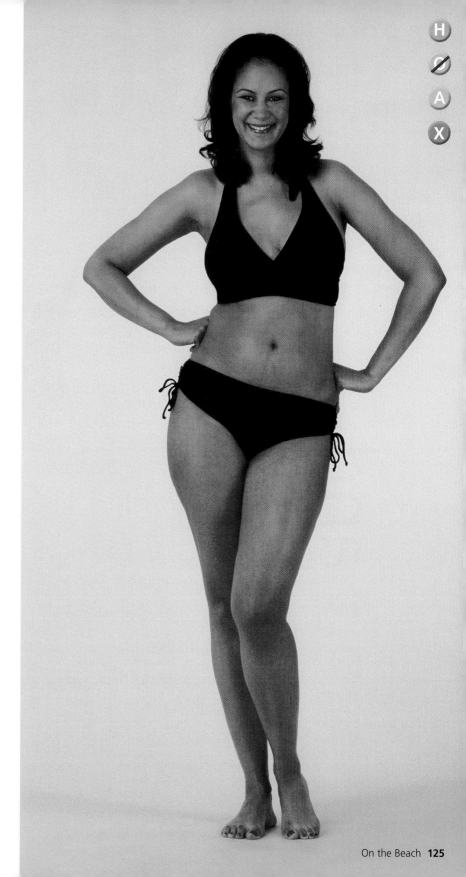

No matter what the
fashion gurus say,
high-cut swimsuits
don't make legs
look lovely when
saddlebags are part
of the picture. Even
though two vertical
lines might flatter
certain figures, they
can't make up for
the rest in this case.

wrap star

You wouldn't wear a skirt this short to the office, but on a bathing suit, it gives legs a good shape. A plunging wrap halter top emphasizes a great-looking bust and waist.

printing
error

You'll know a print is unflattering
the moment you see yourself in the
mirror. And when the waist evapo-
rates and the chest melts into the
rest of your body, swim right away.

print
perfect

Faux skirts can help define the waist and create the illusion of longer legs.

inappropriate

Enough already.

appropriate

The perfect cover-up.

underneath it all

One of the secret pleasures of being a woman is wearing soft, silky lingerie next to your skin. Lingerie isn't just to delight your sweetie; it can also make you feel wonderful and sexy all day long. And when it comes to lingerie, we believe every woman has the inalienable right to wear whatever strikes her fancy in her home and whatever she pleases under her clothes. So there.

Undergarments are the base on which beautiful shapes are built so why deprive yourself of this marvelous opportunity? Lingerie should not only be pretty, it should also be caressingly comfortable while supporting and smoothing our womanly curves.

The options are endless. Footless support hose lets you wear sandals while it evens out lumps and bumps. A full-body suit provides a sleek surface under clingy clothes. And let's not forget the bra—wait until you see what a difference a proper fit makes.

A final note: Underpinnings are a little secret between you and you—but between you and us, wouldn't it be more fun to choose lovely looks? Think about it. You can go around all day humming *I Feel Pretty*, radiating beauty and confidence, and everyone will wonder just what that little secret could be.

your cup
runneth over

If the cups are too small,
the straps don't lift and
the underwire doesn't lie
flat against the chest, you
should burn your bra.

If your breasts stay up and don't pop out—and bulges are nowhere to be seen—your bra is perfect.

the winner's cup

quack quack

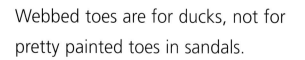

Webbed toes are for ducks, not for
pretty painted toes in sandals.

Wonder of wonders, footless control pantyhose to wear under trousers—with sandals, too.

hello tootsie

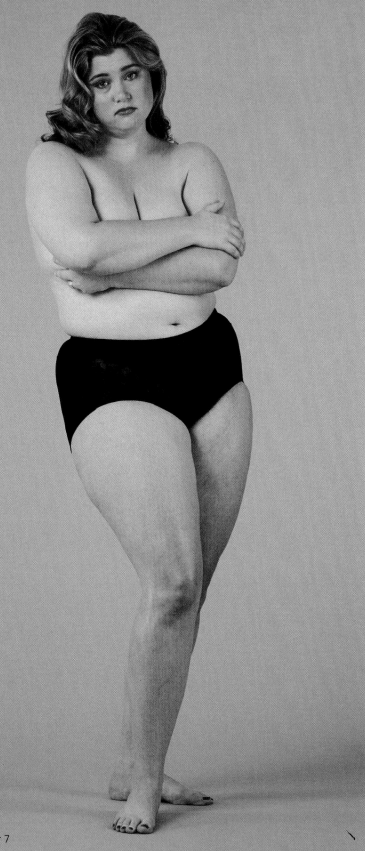

out of
control

Control panties with
panels that have no
control and legs that cut
into your thighs aren't
control panties.

in
control

When the stomach is smooth and there's no bump at the hip/thigh juncture, then you've found a real pair of control panties.

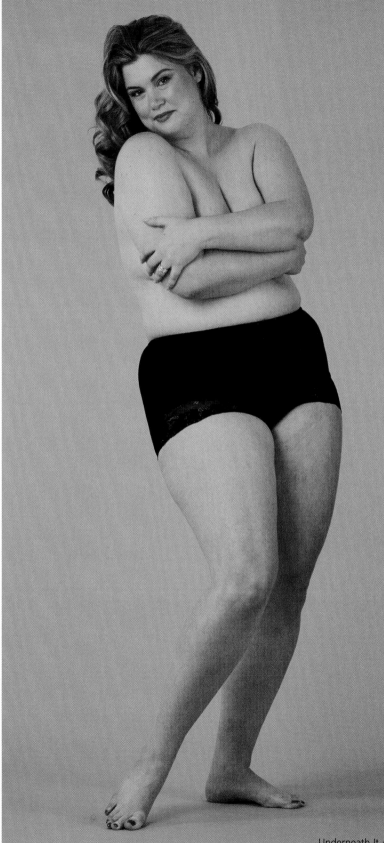

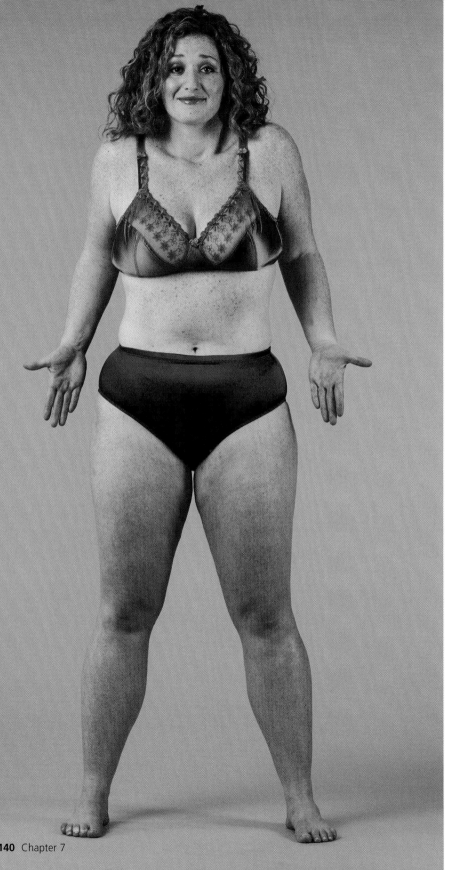

shake, rattle and roll

High-cut control panties
and saddlebags don't
belong together, nor
do tight waistbands
and stomachs.

boy, oh boy, oh boy!

Boy cut legs and
non-constricting
waists don't create
ripples and rolls.

Elasticized French-cut briefs were not made for round tummies and curvy hips.

cut it out

a cut
above

High-cut briefs with light control gently embrace and help erase the hips and stomach.

(P.S. While we are on the subject, always match bras and panties. It's the little things that count, even if you're the only one who knows.)

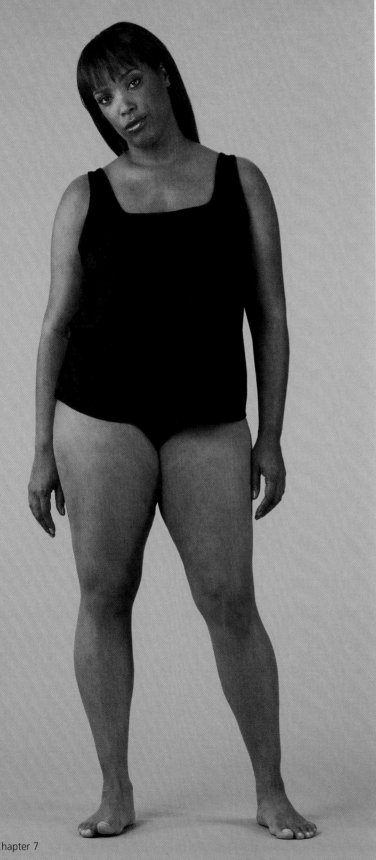

all holds
barred

Camisoles without stretch
might keep you warm, but
they won't hold you in.

getting a hold

Stretch saves the day by
defining the waist and
molding the midriff.

a short bumpy ride

They're called bicycle
shorts, but if they're
too short, your thighs
will get the short end
of the stick and
bulge out all over.

Bicycle shorts
with slightly
raised waists
and long legs
produce enviable
X-shaped figures.

the naked truth

Rubenesque may be ravishing but au naturelle doesn't look pretty as a picture under clingy clothes.

Go all the way in a one-piece
body suit that lifts, supports,
smoothes and streamlines.

supporting evidence

inappropriate

Lumpy, bumpy and frumpy.

Smooth and easy.

appropriate

the final flourish

Accessories are the grand gesture at the end of the show—your big moment to take your basic wardrobe and make it your own. Belts, buckles, bangles, beads, bows...the list goes on and on. Each accessory adds a bit of magic until—poof!—your wardrobe becomes your signature statement.

Madeleine Albright likes big broaches; masses of pearls suited Coco Chanel; Jackie Kennedy loved large, dark sunglasses; Audrey Hepburn shone in silky scarves. Just look what Halle Berry did for a belt slung around her hips in the James Bond flick *Die Another Day*. It's a trick almost any woman can try...with or without the bikini.

You're a gorgeous Rubenesque creature whose body deserves dramatic adornment. Accessories fall into two categories: ditsy (i.e. miniscule) and dramatic (i.e. big and beautiful). Think scale and proportion. When it comes to accessories, bigger is better.

Always try on accessories before you take them home. Stand in front of a full-length mirror to make sure the bag isn't too small, the necklace too delicate, the earrings too boring. Test the colors next to your face. Is that puce and chartreuse scarf really going light up your life?

A final note: Long, unbroken lines make for a longer, lovelier look, since they keep the eye sweeping down in one straight line. Match hose to your shoes if you can. If you like the appearance of a nude leg, shoes should always be darker than the hose. If perchance you weren't blessed with a nice turn at the ankle, avoid ankle straps and opt instead for simple pumps.

blah blah

Tiny earrings are
for tiny women.

Important earrings can illuminate
the face and draw attention up,
up and away from figure flaws.

bling bling

slip
shod

Dark pants
shouldn't hang
around light
shoes.

Dark shoes are shoo-ins for dark trousers.

shoe in

give 'em the boot

Save short boots for long skirts and pants and make sure they don't cut off your circulation.

boot up

You're lookin' good as long as the hem of the skirt meets the top of the boots.

lost in space

Teensy necklaces look even teensier on a voluptuous woman, maybe even ridiculous.

pile it on

You're a big, beautiful woman. Your accessories should be big and beautiful.

baby bracelets

Narrow bangle
bracelets get lost
on ample arms.

Bold statement bangles are in scale with bigger bodies.

beaux bangles

Don't turn a scarf into a turtleneck if you don't have enough neck to stick out.

neck brace

take the plunge

Turn a scarf into a plunging V and—voilà–you have a new blouse and a long neck.

ankles away

If you weren't
around when
they handed out
ankles, don't step
near ankle straps.

going
strapless

Pumps are perfect.

round off

Round glasses make round faces look rounder.

right
angles

Clean, angular frames and
mid-sized lenses sculpt
cherubic faces and play up
gorgeous cheekbones.

bag it

Itty bitty bags belong
on little women.

big bang bag

Large, structured
bags give big
women a big look.

inappropriate

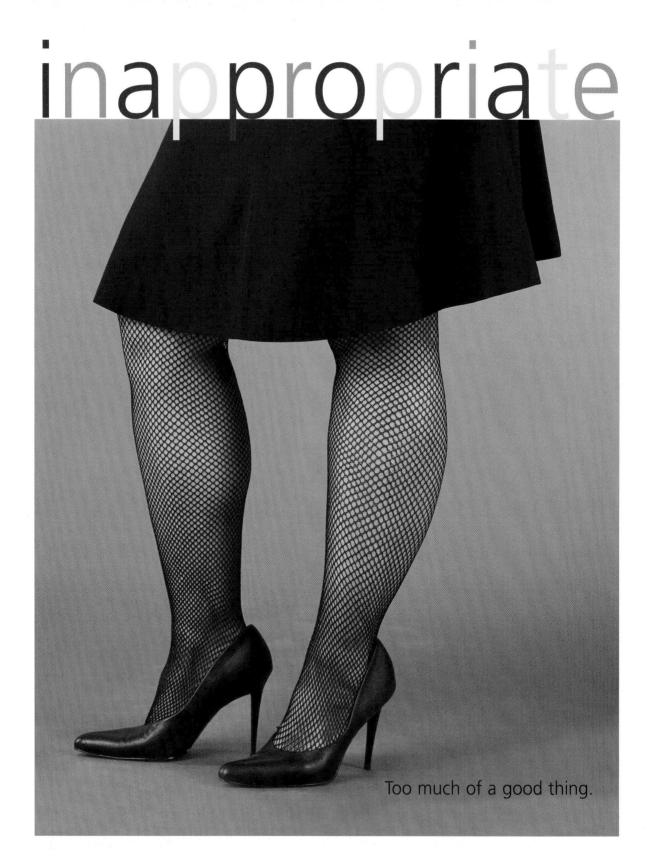

Too much of a good thing.

appropriate

A little dab will do it.

an ode to shopping

In our PJs on the web
Dressed up at the mall
Alone and with friends
For much or for nothing at all

At sales and full price
At noon and at night
To find things we love
And things not quite right

Love it and loathe it
Till we're ready to drop
Take it or leave it
We shop—and can't stop

Now that you know what looks great on you, it's time for the best part: shopping!

More than carrying the clothes we love, our favorite stores help us choose what looks best on us and care more about keeping us as customers than getting the next sale. Quite simply, they make us feel welcome.

We searched all over the country to find the best clothes for this book. Although not every item of clothing looks great on the models in the pictures, all the clothes have been designed to look good on someone.

You need to decide if you're the right someone when you see something you love. Hopefully, we've helped.

Thanks to the stores we love most—**Fashion Bug, Catherines and Lane Bryant**—for understanding that not all women wear size 4, 6 or 8 and for finding clothes that look great on real women.

Also thanks to:
• Emme • Escada • Ellen Tracy • Talbots
• Lands' End • Dana Buchman • Wal-Mart

• Ralph Lauren • Harve Bernard • H&M
• Gap • I.N.C. • Chanel • Manolo Blahnik
• Nine West • Stuart Weitzman • Vivien Goa
• Hanes • Yves Saint Laurent • Nancy Ganz

Kudos to Ford Models, the Goddess division of Model Service Agency, LLC and Wilhelmina Models for finding the beautiful women who graced the pages of *figure it out.*

They are: Karenbeatrice Porcher (pg 13), Tomiko Peirano (pg 14), Kimberly Stout (pg 16), Jordan Tesfay (pg 20), Jessica LaVoie (pg 22), Megan Garcia (pg 24), Bernadett Vajda (pg 126) and Shellie Biviens (pg 144).

Our kisses go to stylist Desiree Konian and assistant stylist Leetoya Casey for their superb fashion sensibilities, to Joe Simon and Karen Panoch for making our models' hair and makeup look natural and gorgeous and to Joanna Goddard for her extraordinary editing and writing talents.

We can't forget to thank Kartell for lending us the stunning Plexiglas "LA MARIE" chairs, designed by Philippe Starck.

—Geri Brin and Tish Jett